Patrick Hall

GANDON EDITIONS

Faust Rising
1983-84   oil on canvas   183 x 305 cm (diptych)   private collection, Dublin

WORKS 12

Patrick Hall

GANDON EDITIONS

WORKS 12 – PATRICK HALL

Published as part of Gandon Editions
WORKS series on the contemporary
visual arts in Ireland (listed on p32).

ISBN   0946641 331

Editor   John O'Regan

Asst Editor   Nicola Dearey
Design   John O'Regan
                © Gandon
Photography   Gerry Farrell
                Gerard Bonus
Production   Gandon
Printing   Betaprint, Dublin

Distributed by Gandon and its
overseas agents.

GANDON EDITIONS LTD

*Gandon Editions gratefully
acknowledges the grant-aiding of
this book as part of the third set of
four titles in the WORKS series by:*

*The Arts Council /
An Chomhairle Ealaíon*

and the support of:

*Gandon Foundation
Betaprint, Dublin*

WORKS 12   PATRICK HALL

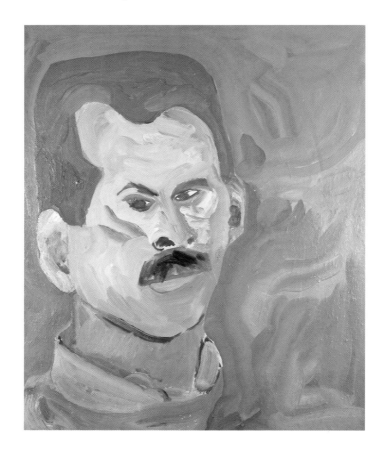

Self-Portrait
1982   oil on canvas   55 x 45 cm   National Self-Portrait Collection

Joe, 9.4.83
1983   oil on canvas   152 x 162 cm   private collection, Dublin

All my painting is an attempt at a literal rendering of a certain thing.

– artist's notes, 1985

I find it practically impossible to talk about painting except in terms of intimacy.

– from speech to Aosdána, 1988

On the canvas I push the paint to the point of disintegration, beyond drawing and almost beyond technique. This induces in me a feeling of being lost. For me lostness is where, in full view of my limitations, I can draw on the necessary energy to paint well.

– notes prepared for Aosdána paper, 1987

Feeling is a radical and a rigorous thing. It is like channelling a river. It can be destructive or productive. In the context of a world that has become a system, feeling can be a door out of the walled space we have built, into another reality. The other reality has its own order, I feel it's a very European thing. The European tradition supplies powerful forms to invest our feelings in. It provides keys into the other reality.

– interview with Andrew Brighton
(Pentonville Gallery, London, 1987)

In the Prado Museum, which I became familiar with over many years, I remember wall after wall of Velazquez, the entire life of the man laid out before me, ambivalent and silent. His companion in these huge rooms was his spiritual elder brother, Titian, the stoic grandeur of whose canvases Charles V had surrounded himself with. Then there was Bosch, scalding in his bleakness. And Goya, the earlier works full of a canny, machiavellian sort of summer, rising, in the later works, to a fierce cry of bitterness and death.

These four painters formed in my mind's eye an ongoing procession of wordless hunger, and the necessity to believe in art that fate forced upon them. They became companions in the self-mutilating isolation of one's sense of oneself and the world, in which one falters in the face of destiny.

– from notes prepared for catalogue statement
Irish Art – The European Dimension, *1990*

PATRICK HALL
in conversation with John Hutchinson

John Hutchinson – In what direction is your painting currently evolving?

Patrick Hall – I'm working on a simpler kind of painting than before. As things stand, I understand 'simpler' to mean an emphasis on figurative painting, paintings of objects – an emphasis that was already evident in my last exhibition. I was trying to pull those pictures back from abstraction, and I just about saved them from disaster. The paintings in that exhibition were abstract to the extent that they went as close to disintegration as I could lead them without actually falling apart. That fine line is central to those works. A sense of being pressed against the edges of reality has always been present in my life, and it had become acute in 1989, when someone very close to me was dying of Aids. I was getting to a point where I didn't think that I could continue to paint at all, and I had to try to find a way out of that impasse, because the paintings weren't good enough to stop painting then.

Did you find a way out?

There was one painting in that exhibition, *The Eye of the Needle*, that was a turning point for me. I had to learn how to approach painting like someone arranging objects on a mantelpiece – the candlesticks, the photographs, everything in its place. Before that, I always worked towards a tension of imbalance, verging on incoherence. In that painting, though, I chose a certain kind of balance and harmony. It looks a bit like a rib-cage, but to me it also resembles a bouquet of flowers. Once I made that decision, the possibility of painting becoming easier began to dawn on me.

Did you seriously contemplate giving up painting?

Yes. I felt that painting, for me, had been an opting out of involvement with the world, and to that extent I saw it as a negative influence. But at the same time it *was* an engagement with the world – with paint as matter and with the materiality of existence itself. So now I'm trying to take painting out of the centre of my life and put it in perspective. That's what I'm involved with at the moment, and it's something I never thought I would be able to contemplate. I've stuck to painting as the one thing that I would

The Flaying of Marsyas II
1984   acrylic on canvas   160 x 240 cm   Municipal Gallery of Modern Art, Dublin

The Flaying of Marsyas VIII
1984   acrylic on canvas   160 x 240 cm   collection of the artist

survive by, or die by. Maybe I'm not destined to become the painter I thought I would be; maybe I'll have to settle for being a good, run-of-the-mill painter. Instead of aiming for perfection, I'm now aiming for completeness, to complete myself – on whatever level that might be. Maybe I need to let go of the idealism that I was brought up with – the high, unspoken perfectionism that developed from my dead parents' seemingly unfinished lives. Painting is only part of life. In the last few months, since I've dislodged the stone of painting from my stomach, it has felt like the release of a flood of water. It is almost as if a well has been unblocked.

Will this free the work to reach greater depths? Or will it diffuse the energy that it contained?

It might diffuse the energy, but I don't think it will. The current of energy that was going into the painting was decreasing anyway, because it was proving to be so difficult. One of the things I've experienced all my life was *difficulty* – when I got up in the morning I assumed everything was going to be arduous. I can't take that any more, even if that means getting rid of painting in the process. I want to abandon difficulty. I want to make the paintings simpler. I want to make my life simpler and more enjoyable. I don't mind if I end up painting flowers in a vase, like Manet did in his old age. I've no more ambitions with regard to painting – I want to excise perfectionism, and just to paint.

Most artists seem to consider their talent to be potentially infinite.

That's what I used to think. I assumed that you had to think like that to achieve quality in the work. It is the opposite now. In order for the work to carry new energy, it has to cease being the sole or dominant object in my existence.

In your paintings are you trying to balance thinking with sensation – the head with the body?

You can't separate the wisdom of the mind from that of the body. My hand has the brush in it and the brush does the work. Afterwards you bring in the mind, and that's what refines the painting. But in the making of a painting the hand is everything. I try to work with that kind of faith in my hand – I believe the hand knows everything; it's the wisdom of matter. And matter has been here much longer than man.

You've always had difficulty with your 'hand' – you haven't a natu-

ral technical facility. But your awkwardness lends a perilous edge to the images.

Let me go back to how I grew up. This burden – a sense of disso- ciation from the body, from the material world around me – was something I inherited from my family. My father especially, whose background was Unionist, found himself, after the War of Indep- endence, in a social and political world with which he was entirely disenchanted. I think he was an embittered man, and he rather cut himself off from the world around him. So when I was growing up I felt isolated and vulnerable, and I started to build high walls around myself, finding pleasure in solitary pursuits such as gar- dening, and developing an interest in mysticism and other hermetic areas. Eventually I ended up with painting as a way of dealing with the world. It was solitary, but it was *material*. It gave me meaning. What I'm doing now is trying to make things simpler, because life is so complicated for me that I can't carry any longer the burden of meaning. You're right: I can think and write more readily than I can paint. Painting doesn't come easily to me. But now I have to bring some joy into the painting; it has to be some- thing I look forward to doing. Painting isn't something that should be an onerous task – it's not a stone that I have to roll up to the top of a hill.

Are you saying that you elected to paint because of the sheer 'materiality' of the process?

Yes, I think so. Painting saved me from the abstract, from the unworldly.

You make painting sound like a form of psychotherapy. It is as if you've used painting as a means to come to terms with the diffi- culties of life, and now that it no longer serves that function you're tempted to reject it.

If I couldn't use painting in the transformation of my life, in my own engagement with existence, I wouldn't have any reason to paint. I can see that painting might at some point become irrelevant to me, but at the moment I don't see that as likely. Painting gives me a thread of joy in my daily life. And while it isn't just therapy, it has to function within the parameters of my own history and fate.

Is it coincidental that there has been an increasing thickness of paint – of matter – in the paintings of the last few years?

It's very difficult to bring meaning into paintings, and I have to use

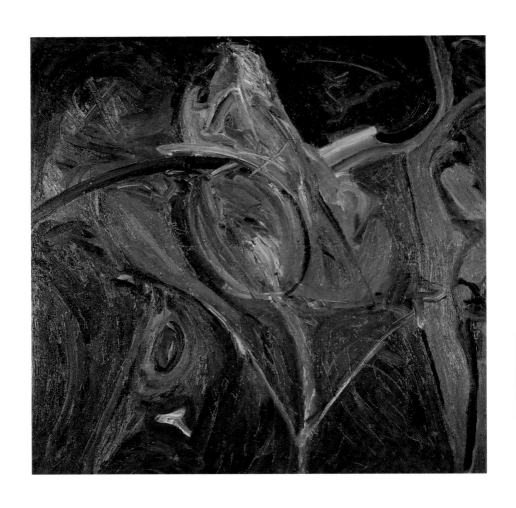

My Mother in the Garden at Glentara
1986-87   oil on canvas   152 x 157 cm   private collection, Cork

Flowers on the Table
1988   oil on canvas   152 x 157 cm   private collection, Cork

a lot of paint to do so. It's only in the very last instant that I manage to bring something out of the painting, and it involves all the paint that I put on the canvas. I find a lot of my earlier paintings very thin. I was looking for something that I hadn't yet found, which turned out to be the scooping of paint out of tins and putting it onto canvases. That led to all the muck, the greyness, the lack of colour and drawing and so forth. Maybe when I'm more expert – if I ever do become more expert – I'll require less matter to achieve the same result. But then, in my relative incompetence, that was the only way I could bring some light out of the canvases. You rub and you rub; you scrape and you scrape; and suddenly some kind of resemblance begins to come out at you from the canvas.

What kind of resemblance?

You don't know until it appears. It's a presence, the presence of the painting.

How do you know when an image is resolved?

I'm not sure that I ever do know.

It's interesting that you use the word 'resemblance'. I assume that you don't mean literal resemblance – is it a reflection, at a particular point in time, of a set of experiences, memories, and responses to the world?

Yes. It's a kind of correspondence to a set of experiences. In one sense you create experience *in* a painting, but in another you don't – you're actually revealing experience that's already experienced, bringing the past into the present, and abandoning it in the creation of the present. At the same time there's a moment of recognition which implies a memory of the past, which until that point has remained unacknowledged. At a certain point it is articulated, released. That's the moment of recognition. That's when you know you've made a painting. That's a moment of joy. The happiness of that moment comes from the feeling of release.

Your subject-matter has become less literal. It used to be autobiographical, but recently it seems to have shifted to a concern with metaphors and symbols.

In the early days my paintings reflected my daily life – they were portraits of friends, still-lifes and so on. Then I became interested in Marsyas and Faust – an area of living that is mythical, fated, and, at the same time, part of everyday existence. So I began to explore areas that I had never investigated before and I discovered that I had no language that could articulate those experiences. My paintings became less image-centred and more 'abstract'. In actual fact though, they were just as 'real' as the still-lives that I was painting in the 'sixties. They were dealing with obsessions that I had – releasing them into the outside world.

Some of your current images, while apparently 'real' and specific, are oddly symbolic. I'm thinking of paintings like The Boxer. *They seem to be charged with a multitude of associations.*

I'm no longer willing to go into my own entrails in order to find something to paint – I need something to happen to me, an image to strike me, and to interact with it. It is through this interaction that I make paintings. My painting is no longer a solitary experience; it is a form of communication, on a lot of different levels, with the outside world. The world of boxing is a sort of idealised world for me, and it is also a very sexual one. My father boxed when he was a young man.

The oils seem to be more abstract and internal; the works on paper are based on simple figurative images. Can you explain the difference between them?

These days I try to work 'blind'. I like the idea of working in the dark, so I can trust myself more – I can't quite see what I'm doing. I'm trying to induce a feeling of safety and trust in myself. In some of the recent works on paper there is more of that trust, which means that they're the result of a happier and easier process of creation. I'm trying to bring themes into my paintings, and all of the works on paper that you're referring to had themes – a deer, a mirror, a story, or something. This easier, happier painting has come about gradually. As I say, it really boiled down to trust, to trusting my hand. You have to trust your own body, because your body has a memory far deeper than your head – and if you can actually invest your energy in all the wisdom that lies dormant in the body, and specifically in your hand, then you're away. I would like to bring the simple story-telling of the works on paper onto the canvases, but it is taking time.

Do you consider abstraction to be a kind of false simplicity?

It sidesteps the ordinary. Life has been complicated for me. I've been drawn into a cycle of complication. I'm attracted to abstraction, but I can't get there in a single jump. To me it's akin to a life of

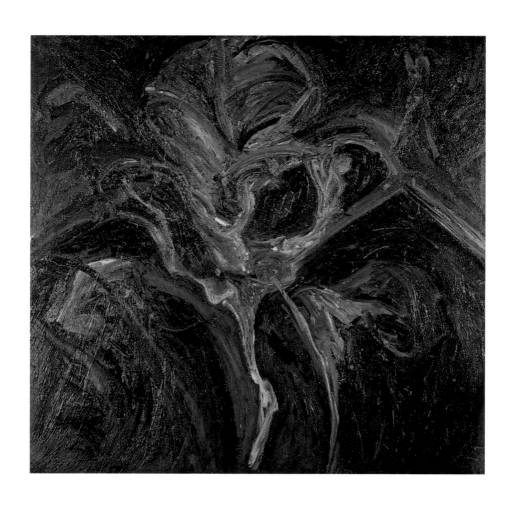

The Eye of the Needle
1987   oil on canvas   152 x 157 cm   private collection, Cork

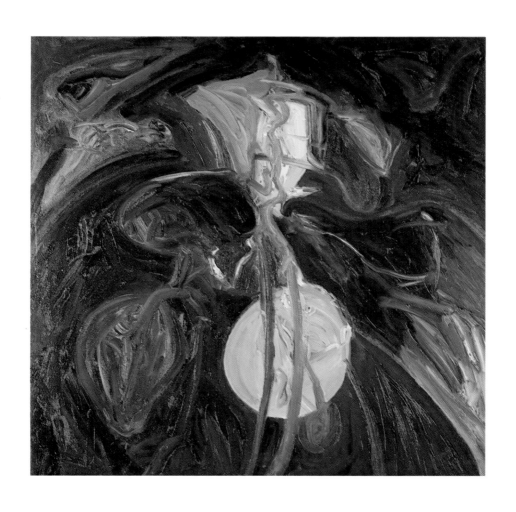

Heart
1986-87   oil on canvas   152 x 157 cm   private collection, Cork

pure spirit – it suggests that life as an angel might be better than life as a human being. I'm not an angel so I have to work out my own experiences through my own body, my own memory, and the interaction between all them.

Weren't many of these complications self-created?

To a certain extent, yes – but I don't think I had any choice in the matter.

Do you regret them?

No, I don't. I wish that my life had been simpler, that it hadn't been so difficult. I'm thinking of the self-destructive tendencies I once had: I wish I hadn't had to flagellate myself for so long in order to reach the point where I find myself now. But I had no choice, and to that extent I'm glad that I took the path that I did because I've never been happier than I am now. And if it took all that to achieve this, then I have no regrets at all.

But you still aspire to simplicity and harmony? Much of your work would seem to suggest that you revel in pain and anxiety.

Simplicity and harmony – yes. As for the rest, I paint what I have lived, incoherence and all. One accepts eventually one's own experience. You asked why I had to use so much paint on my canvas. It is because of my incompetence. Similarly, the complications in my life have been due to incompetence. I didn't have any other road to take.

Is there anyone who has the simplicity and depth to which you aspire?

Titian. He was a person whose life was full of anxiety and trouble, but one part of him always kept contact with a changeless world. I like that changelessness, because it gives his work a kind of serenity, which is a doorway into another world. His paintings, at best, just glow. The portraits, for instance, are wonderful: they're straightforward humanist images which mark the beginning of the solitude of modern consciousness. I love Velazquez and Goya as well. For them, painting was part of something greater.

How about Expressionism – and Francis Bacon?

The best of Expressionism, and the best of Bacon too, is involved with a world which is outside the world of painting. I identify with painters whose work comes from something other than a preoccupation with aesthetics – in other words, when their painting is *driven* by need. They're working out their own destinies in painting. There are very few painters who do that. Bacon, of course, and Munch and Nolde, Giacometti and Auerbach. I am inspired by painters who had to work hard over a long time to put together what they achieved, who were not obviously 'gifted' painters. The very personal, enclosed lives of these artists, illuminated by the culture of art, yet far from the 'art world', contain great depth and warmth, and at the same time have an epic quality. It is this enclosed aspect that is important to me, and I don't mean esoteric necessarily. Ingmar Bergman said, 'Art is a very small thing'.

How would you counter the criticism that your kind of painting is a very egotistical form of art?

It could be described as egotistical, I suppose. I *am* full of myself, I guess, because my self is the touchstone of my own reality – but I paint in response to the world around me and in an attempt to speak to it, because I can't separate the world from myself. I *am* preoccupied with my own destiny, even though I'm not yet quite sure what it is. And that absorbs all my attention. But in any case, since we are all part of the world, if we can come to terms with our own destinies, we're strengthening the relation of the world to itself and of every individual in the world to each other. If I were to decide to try to make my paintings contribute to the healing of whatever malaise I might choose to focus on, I could only do so by dealing with my own malaise. If I can set that to rights, I'm making the only contribution an individual can make to healing the world. I'm not a Savonarola, a psychiatrist or a social worker. If an individual can live in harmony with himself, he is contributing to the harmony of the world.

Is yours a humanist or a religious view of the world?

I'm not sure that there's a difference, actually. I think the dividing line between the human and the divine is non-existent. Divinity is the completion of humanity. My idea of eternity is completeness, wholeness. The more you advance towards completeness, the more divine you become – if that is the correct word.

Do you think that we leave behind matter and physicality when we die? If so, is that a prospect that you anticipate with joy?

Matter, which preoccupies me so much, is the only way I can prepare for the next world. But I don't think that we do leave behind

High Road
1991   ink and acrylic on paper   56 x 85 cm   collection of the artist

Orange Hill
1991   ink and acrylic on paper on board   70 x 100 cm   collection of the artist

all matter – matter is unending. I'm not sure that there is a matter-less, ethereal existence ahead of us. I'm not sure that the distinction between matter and spirit is absolute. The present task for me, in being willing to let go of painting, is to retain the motivation to paint. The process of letting go is crucial to the freedom on which painting is founded. The willingness to let go of painting, for me, is part of the process of dying. It may even be letting go of immortality. It is a dilemma I hope to paint through. In a way it is the end of a journey, the completion of a circle, which began when I discovered that art could be an alternative to reality.

Do you face the future with optimism?

Yes I do. It's taken a long time for that to happen, though. And I have to be optimistic if I'm to go on painting.

July 1992

ON THE PAINTING *THE RISING OF FAUST* BY PATRICK HALL
Michael O'Brien

1

He's moving through an ocean of air
Four figures as one.
Screws and nails vaguely propel him,
While his head is so full
It falls away, it loses its knowledge of shape,
It's so full of the burnt red land
And the red sky burnt by his movement.

On massive thighs
Through the metalled air –
A shredded musculature.

2

He was discovered out of a sixty square foot canvas,
The world he found himself in.
He is bowed, lurching, forgetting nothing in his elephantine head.
His elephantine head is unable to forget.

Around him the air explodes.
The shrapnel of experience and the lacerations of time
Have shredded his musculature.
One rigid black rod fixes too stiffly and places him,
Supports and earths him,
A lightning conductor to relieve him.

Aeons meet in him.
No face can be put upon
This figure escaping his fall.

3

Through the thickness of the paint
He's drawing everything in two.

His cauldron bowels,
His plucked and cauterized genitals
Support the subplot upper torso,
Somewhere between Apollo and the beast.
He is Faust in hell.

Boxer
1991   ink and acrylic on paper   56 x 85 cm   collection of the artist

The Burning Mountain
1992   ink and acrylic on paper   56 x 85 cm   collection of the artist

Patrick Hall
photo: John Searle, 1992

PATRICK HALL

1935   Born near Roscrea in Co Tipperary
1958-60   Studied at Chelsea School of Art, Central School of Art, London
          Member of Aosdána
          Lives and works in Dublin

Solo Exhibitions

1990   Fenderesky Gallery at Queen's, Belfast. . Catalogue.
1988   Todd Gallery, London
1985/89   Temple Bar Gallery, Dublin
1985/87   Pentonville Gallery, London. Catalogue.
1980/83   Lincoln Gallery, Dublin

Selected Group Exhibitions

1992   Fenderesky Gallery at Queen's, Belfast
          Boyle Arts Festival, Co Roscommon
1991   Jack Rutberg Gallery, Los Angeles
          In A State, Kilmainham Gaol, Dublin. Catalogue.
          Parable Island, Bluecoat Gallery, Liverpool. Catalogue.
1990   Cologne International Art Fair, Fenderesky Gallery
          Irish Art of the Eighties, Douglas Hyde Gallery Dublin. Catalogue
          Irish Art – European Dimension, RHA Gallagher Gallery, Dublin.
          Catalogue.
1988   *Death*, Cambridge Darkroom and Kettle's Yard Open Exhibition
1986   *4 Irish Expressionists*, Northeastern University / Boston College
1984   *The October Exhibition*, Temple Bar Gallery, Dublin. Catalogue.
1983   *Making Sense*, Project Arts Centre, Dublin – Arts Council
          Touring Exhibition. Catalogue.

Selected Bibliography

1991   'Critic's Choice' by Robert Clark, *The Guardian,* 16 Feb, 14 Mar
          Keeping the Faith, radio Interview by Kevin O'Kelly, RTE Radio 1
1990   'Myth and Mystification' by John Hutchinson; *A New Tradition –*
          Irish Art of the Eighties, Douglas Hyde Gallery, Dublin
1987   'Life Lines', by Aidan Dunne; and
          '*Heart* and other recent paintings', by Andrew Brighton;
          catalogue essays, Pentonville Gallery, London
1986   *Religion and Religiosity* by Donald Kuspit, symposium at
          Museum of Fine Arts, Boston
          'Creation and Recreation' by Tim Norris; catalogue of *4 Irish*
          Expressionists, Boston
1983   'A Talk with the Painter Patrick Hall' by Michael O'Brien; *The*
          Beau, no.3, Dublin
          'Patrick Hall' by Henry J Sharpe; catalogue of *Making Sense*,
          Project Arts Centre, Dublin

The Heart of the Forest
1991   ink and acrylic on paper   56 x 85 cm   private collection, Barcelona

Ancestors
1990-91   oil on canvas   152 x 157 cm   Irish Museum of Modern Art

THE WORKS SERIES

edited by John O'Regan

to be continued . . .

GANDON EDITIONS